KEEPING CHICKENS

A Practical Journal for Life Out Here

Skyhorse Publishing, Inc.

Portions of this book were previously published as *Proven Techniques for Keeping Healthy Chickens* (978-1-5107-3720-4), *50 Do-It-Yourself Projects for Keeping Chickens* (978-1-5107-3175-2), and *The Joy of Keeping Chickens* (978-1-63220-467-7).

Copyright © 2019 by Hollan Publishing

All rights reserved. No part of this publication may be reproduced or stored in a retrieval system or transmitted in any form or by any means, whether electronic, mechanical photocopying, recording or other kind, without the prior permission in writing of the owners. All inquiries should be addressed to Skyhorse Publishing, 307 West 36th Street, 11th Floor, New York, NY 10018.

Skyhorse Publishing books may be purchased in bulk at special discounts for sales promotion, corporate gifts, fund-raising, or educational purposes. Special editions can also be created to specifications. For details, contact the Special Sales Department, Skyhorse Publishing, 307 West 36th Street, 11th Floor, New York, NY 10018 or info@skyhorsepublishing.com.

Skyhorse® and Skyhorse Publishing® are registered trademarks of Skyhorse Publishing, Inc.®, a Delaware corporation.

Visit our website at www.skyhorsepublishing.com.

10 9 8 7 6 5 4 3 2 1

Library of Congress Cataloging-in-Publication Data is available on file.

Cover design by Melissa Gerber
Cover art provided by Shutterstock.com

ISBN: 978-1-5107-5096-8

Printed in China

This journal belongs to

_____

{ Chickens are communal animals that live and thrive in a flock. *Never keep just one chicken by herself.*

{ The general rule of thumb is that you need a *minimum of* 2.5 square feet of space per bird if they free-range during the day or 14 square feet of space per bird if they are always confined.

> Protect coops from drafts in winter; cold air should *never be blowing* on chickens in the coop.

> When the weather turns cold, feed your chickens snacks at bedtime, such as corn or other scratch grains. *Digesting food at night* keeps a chicken's metabolism going and ensures the chickens have enough calories to burn all night.

{ *Ventilation* is necessary for the air quality of the chicken coop. If you build a coop from scratch, make sure you plan vents along the top of the walls for proper airflow.

{ Tall grasses can cause problems for chickens. Cut grass to *a few inches* in height before letting chickens graze.

{ To *make your own* nest boxes, use plastic bins, laundry baskets, cat litter boxes, buckets, or wooden crates.

{ Add food-grade diatomaceous earth powder and herbs to nesting material to help *deter pests*.

> Give hens a *quiet, secluded environment* for laying eggs to reduce the effects of stress and make your chickens more productive.

{ When chickens sleep, they go into a very *deep trance*. It's a wonder they don't fall off their roost!

{ Whenever possible, keep your chickens from sleeping on the floor. Provide a *roost bar* to give them a feeling of security.

{ Chickens appreciate *a place to rest* during the day. Placing outdoor perches and roosts around the chicken run or in the yard lets them rest up off the ground.

{ Add 2 tablespoons of *apple cider vinegar* to your chicken's water a few times a week to keep their digestive tracts healthier, reduce their susceptibility to intestinal parasites, and strengthen their immune systems.

{ Place *fresh mint leaves* in the coop to calm the hens during laying.

{ Mint, lavender, thyme, and other *aromatic herbs* are great natural insect repellents to use in the coop.

{ Put a *large tree limb* in your chicken run. The chickens will enjoy pecking for the insects living in the branches.

{ Dandelion gives eggs a *rich yellow* egg yolk color. Provide some plants for your chickens to peck at or add it to their feed.

{ Some common garden plants that can cause *toxicity* in chickens are azaleas, buttercup, clematis, foxglove, henbane, honeysuckle, iris, rhododendron, and sweet pea.

 { Chickens love *spicy peppers* and their seeds!

{ Add a *chicken wire cover* to your chicken run to protect them from hawks, owls, and other flying predators.

{ The best wire fencing for coop security is *hardware cloth*. It does not bend as easily as chicken wire and is welded, making it a stronger system for keeping out predators.

> When constructing a chicken run, make sure the wire extends a few inches *underground* to prevent predators from digging under the fence.

{ When planning a chicken run, consider adding plants, structures, or other objects that will provide shade. *Shady areas* for food and water will protect chickens from overheating in hot weather.

{ To *control mud in your chicken run,* add wood chips, wood fiber, straw, mulch, stones, or pine needle straw.

{ When the ground in the chicken area builds up with bedding, dirt, spilled feed, and straw, it should be re-graded and returned to a somewhat *gentle slope* toward the downward side of the yard.

{ Use a *tiller* to stir up the dirt in the chicken area and make it drain better.

{ Add a *layer of clean straw* to the chicken run to clean off the chickens' feet before they walk back into the coop.

To express dominance, chickens puff up their feathers, flap their wings, jump on each other, peck, squawk, and more.

{ Chickens love to have fun and enjoy *new experiences*. Adding boredom busters, such as swings and perches, to the run will help chickens stay healthy.

{ A *cabbage piñata* will keep your chickens busy for hours! Place a cabbage head in a metal hanging basket (remove any planting moss the basket may have come with) and hang it at beak height.

{ Build a *trough snack bar* for your chickens. Construct a slightly raised bed and plant herbs, salad greens, grass, or edible flowers.

{ Dust bathing is how a chicken cleans its body and feathers, and the process is essential to the *good health* of the bird.

{ Chickens take *dust baths* to repel and eliminate lice, mites, and other skin irritants. Believe it or not, all that dirt is good for the chickens!

{ To make a dust bath area for your chickens, you'll need *four ingredients*: dry dirt, wood ash (from a fire pit or fireplace; do not use ash from treated charcoal), food-grade diatomaceous earth (which dehydrates any insects), and builder's sand (to make the mixture light and fluffy).

{ Repurpose an old *patio umbrella* to add shade to a sunny chicken run.

{ Place nontoxic garden plants, such as *rose bushes, sunflowers, and marigolds*, around the perimeter of the chicken run. The flock will snack on the leaves and blossoms that poke through the fence.

Initial *signs of illness* in a chicken can include a droopy appearance, standing off from the flock, lack of appetite, absence of egg production, swelling, or discolored or pale comb or wattles. Seek veterinary help if you see these signs in a member of your flock.

Chickens will hide the signs of illness so that they don't look like easy prey. It also protects them from getting picked on by flock members. You'll need to *observe your flock closely* for signs of illness.

{ Items to keep in your chicken *first aid kit* include saline solution, scissors, disposable gloves, bandages, gauze, tape, tweezers, cotton swabs, syringe, and wound care spray.

{ When caring for chickens, *clean drinking water* is a top priority. Hens won't lay eggs as well if they become dehydrated.

A chicken produces approximately *2 cubic feet of manure* per year.

{ The average chicken eats approximately *1/2 cup of feed* per day.

> Cold weather is the appropriate time for feeding your flock extra energy foods like *corn, winter squash, and pumpkin.*

{ The *average age* at which a hen starts laying eggs is six months.

{ To encourage chickens to *come home at night,* try leaving a battery-powered lantern, solar-powered garden light, or an LED night-light in the coop to draw them inside.

> In addition to a diet of layer feed, it's fun to bring chickens *table scraps and garden goodness,* such as watermelon, blueberries, strawberries, raisins, or corn.

{ *Free-ranging birds* are less likely to get bored or fight with each other, tend to lay more nutrient-rich eggs, and require less feed than confined chickens.